scissors so as not to damage my good fabric scissors. Remove the paper backing and position the appliqué pieces onto your background fabric. When satisfied fuse using a dry hot iron until the glue is well melted and the fabric is secure.

You still need to edge your appliqué particularly if planning to wash the articles. You can use a hand buttonhole stitch as I have done, a machine buttonhole stitch, satin stitch or other fancy stitch to do this.

Stitching

Use 1 or 2 strands of DMC stranded cotton following the photographs and stitch keys for colour placement or choose your own colours and threads. A size 7 or 8 crewel or Applibond needle to stitch and a 6-8" embroidery hoop is recommended. Place the fabric into the hoop having the fabric firm but not stretched. Use the stitch guide below for assistance with the individual stitches. Begin and end with knots, as the pellon will 'hide' any threads on the back of your stitchery.

Backstitch   French knot   Running stitch

Bias Strips

There are several ways to make bias strips for the stems and vines used in this book.

• You can purchase premade bias tape in several widths and colours with or without fusible strips on the back.

• You can use a bias maker and make your own strips, again with or without fusible strips on the back.

This is the method I used:

Cut strips of fabric $3/4$" wide. (if the stems are going to be straight you can cut strips on the straight grain, if they are to be used for curved vines then you need to cut on the true bias - 45° to the selvedge).

Place two needles or pins into an ironing board or similar an irons width apart.

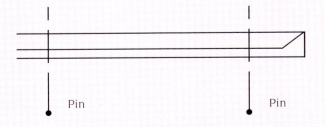

Pin   Pin

The amount of needle showing in the middle section needs to be the finished width of your binding. Lay your strip right side down and fold the top and bottom edges in. Feed the end of the strip under the middle section of both needles. Sit your iron with steam setting on down in between the pins on top of the folded strip and gently pull the strip through steaming down the folds as it passes.

If you want fusible strips on the back just cut $1/8$" wide strips of vliesofix fusible webbing and fuse them along the back of the bias strips. Remove the paper, position on your quilt and fuse to secure until stitching.

Hot fix crystal embellishments

Throughout the book I have added embellishments to the projects using Hot fix Crystals and Nailheads. These can be applied using a special tailor made applicator or with a household iron. If using an applicator follow the enclosed instructions. If using an iron place the crystals into position and use the tip of the iron to melt the glue taking care not to scorch your fabric.

Embellishments are great fun but optional!! You could use beads, sew on crystals or sequins, metallic or rayon threads, knot or satin stitches in place of the hot fix crystals. All projects will still look divine without them.

Layering your quilt

Press your backing fabric and quilt top carefully. Lay backing fabric right side down onto a table or flat surface. Tape the edges to secure the backing fabric having it taught but not stretched. Smooth your wadding centrally over the backing fabric and then lay the quilt top centrally on to the top. The backing fabric and wadding should be larger than the quilt top by at least 1"/2.5cm on all sides. Do not trim it at this stage as you want a full binding. Smooth out any wrinkles and pin, hand or glue baste the three layers together. Or you may like to use your own preferred method of layering.

Quilting your quilt or project

Once your project is layered and secured with pins, basting thread or basting spray you can now quilt it. Use a walking foot for straight line quilting and a darning foot for free motion quilting. You can use matching threads, contrasting threads, invisible threads or specialty threads to quilt. Quilt a long stabilising row in each direction first. Then complete any straight line quilting before ending with free motion quilting such as stippling or meandering to fill sections. Secure the beginnings and endings of all threads. I have given more extensive ideas for quilting each individual project throughout the book.

Binding

In all of the projects I have cut binding strips $2\frac{1}{2}''$ wide unless otherwise stated on either the straight or bias grain of the fabric to give a finished $\frac{1}{2}''$ double bind. Join your strips to make one long strip. It is best to use mitred joins to lessen the bulk. Press your binding strips in half wrong sides together to give a double layer. If not applying piping use a $\frac{1}{4}''$ machine foot and attach to the right side of your quilt top mitring the corners. Have the binding edges level with the edges of the quilt top, not the wadding or backing fabric which is larger. Join the start and finish with a mitred join also to lessen bulk and hide the join. Trim corners and the edge of the wadding and backing to $\frac{1}{2}''$ from the stitching line. Turn the binding to the back of the quilt, pin and slipstitch covering the stitching line, using a thread which matches the backing fabric.

Mitred joins

Fold all your strips in half and lay them on a straight line on your cutting mat with the ends crossing the 45° line. Cut off all ends at the 45° angle.

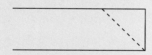

Place two strip ends right sides together and stitch with a $\frac{1}{4}''$ seam taking care not to stretch the bias seam.

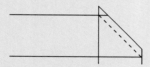

Hanging sleeve

Whether a small or large wallhanging or quilt it is always easier to attach a hanging sleeve before you bind it. Cut a strip of fabric approximately 9" wide and the same width as your finished quilt. Turn in a double hem at both short ends and stitch. Press the strip in half wrong sides together. Open out and machine stitch a row $\frac{1}{4}''$ from this fold line. Refold and position the sleeve with the stitched line against the quilt back and with raw edges even along the top of the back of your quilt. Baste. When attaching the binding to the front you will secure the sleeve in this stitch line. After handstitching the binding to the back of your quilt you can handstitch the sleeve along the bottom edge by slightly lifting the sleeve and handstitching along the previously stitched line with the thread going through the backing fabric and batting only.

These are the thread and pencils colours I have used for all projects in the book. Mark this page as you will need to refer to it often. You of course may choose your own colours to match your chosen fabrics. For convenience this can also be found inside the back cover and on the tear-out design sheets.

DMC Stranded cottons

1. 155 - Forget me knot blue
2. 601 - Dark cranberry
3. 603 - Cranberry
4. 604 - Light cranberry
5. 729 - Medium old gold
6. 772 - Very light yellow green
7. 801 - Dark coffee brown
8. 838 - Very dark beige brown
9. 840 - Medium beige brown
10. 841 - Light beige brown
11. 961 - Dark rusty rose
12. 3013 - Light khaki green
13. 3746 - Dark blue violet

**Derwent colour pencils -
Artist or studio pencil range**

A. 0500 - Straw yellow
B. 1800 - Rose Pink
C. 2000 - Crimson Lake
D. 2100 - Rose madder lake
E. 2500 - Dark violet
F. 2600 - Light violet
G. 2700 - Blue violet lake
H. 4400 - Water green
I. 4500 - Mineral green
J. 4600 - Emerald green
K. 4800 - May green
L. 5100 - Olive Green

colour is the key

...times in life we are unexpectedly blessed. My surprise came along in 2004 and although it changed our life plans we would could never picture our family without her. So with three beautiful girls in the house I cannot help myself when it comes to pretty things and spoiling them with special goodies made as memories to treasure. Every day seems to be another pyjama party now...

Making beautiful things for special little girls, (and our bigger girls) is what we get most pleasure and satisfaction from. The sparkle in the eye when you hand over a quilt made just for them is a special moment in life. We all, as stitchers have those little girl dreams in us and making pretty things makes us feel special again too. Mums, Grandmas, Sisters, Aunties, I am sure you all have someone in your lives who loves pretties and who you love to spoil with your stitching projects.

Along with the main quilt 'Tilly and friends' I have included two lovely but quicker coordinating quilts and the instructions to make matching doona cover, pillowcase and curtains. You may choose to complete just one project or a whole room! Or use the design elements in your own projects, there are many ways to use them. A wallhanging design, and dilly bag complete the range and will keep you stitching for months!

So Matilda May, my special surprise has been spoilt by her adoring sisters and everyone around her as we worked on these projects for you all to share and use to spoil yourself and yours... I do hope they help you to live your dream and create lifetime memories.

Once again a huge thankyou to my wonderful understanding family who love to share in my dreams and support me through everything, especially Pyjama Parties! And to my loyal stitching friends for encouraging me to keep creating beautiful designs to share with you all.

Hele

contents

Designs by Helen Stubbings
Artwork by Katey McConachy
Photography by Richard Barren

ISBN 0-9757444-1-0
Pyjama Party: With Tilly and Friends

hugs n kisses

first things first

- All seams throughout the book are ¼". Seam allowances are included in the sizes given in the cutting instructions.

- Requirements given are based on 100% cotton fabric, non-directional, 42" or 110cm wide.

- The projects are easiest cut and most accurately made using a rotary blade cutter, ruler and cutting mat. Templates may be made if you do not have this equipment.

- Fabrics are placed right sides together unless otherwise stated in the project instructions.

- I have used a lightweight fusible pellon (very thin batting) behind some of my stitcheries throughout the book. This gives a lovely quilted effect and hides any knots or travelling of threads behind the fabric. Check manufacturer's instructions for usage but generally a warm to hot steam iron is used to fuse the layers together. Place the fabric on top of the pellon with the glue dots or rough side uppermost. Press from the fabric side. Use an appliqué mat or pressing mat to protect your iron and your stitchery. You may choose not to use it or instead hand or glue baste a non fusible pellon.

- Read through all instructions before beginning a project.

- I recommend and use the Folk Art brand of Textile medium by Plaid for sealing your Colourqué™. Other brands will work but please test on a scrap before using.

- I recommend and list colours for Derwent Artists or Studio pencils throughout the book. Again, other brands will work but test first.

- Steam a Seam® has been used in the Dilly Bag project. There are two types and either is fine. It is a fusible webbing product but has the advantage of not fraying if the edges have not been stitched, hence its use for 3 dimensional flowers.

Fabric choice

As the projects in this book are somewhat 'scrappy' there are many ways to choose your fabrics. If you think you would like to make them all then I suggest you begin by choosing 3 colours and start collecting. Look for lights and darks in each colour, textures, patterns, stripes, spots, small floral prints which all coordinate. Purchase fat or skinny quarters of each. I would suggest at least 15 greens, 14 pinks and 12 purples.

You would then need to choose specific fabrics for larger requirements like borders, stitchery backgrounds, curtaining, sheeting, piping, backing and binding as per the individual project instructions.

Tracing

Use a light box, window or light source and a soft mechanical lead pencil or blue water erasable pen (only if you are not colouring). Tape the design (you may wish to photocopy this from the pattern sheet first) onto your light source. Centre the background fabric over the design, tape to secure. Carefully trace the design. You may not need to trace every little detail. For example a line for a leaf or a dot for a flower may suffice and then follow your book as you stitch. Alternatively you may have purchased iron on transfers for the designs. All transfer instructions are on the sheets.

Colourqué™

Using a warm to hot dry iron attach freezer paper to the back of your stitchery design. This helps to stabilise the fabric whilst colouring. Using the colouring guide and photographs colour all indicated areas of your stitchery panels. Colour quite darkly and keep your pencils sharp to get a good fine line and even blending. If blending two colours on a leaf or petal for example, fill the whole shape with the lighter colour and then 'feather' the darker colour over the top from the outside edge in towards the centre of the shape. Do not worry if your blending lines show as these will 'blend' whilst you stitch. You may choose to use just flat colours with no blending at all and this too will look great. Now, if you like the depth of colouring as it is now, then you need to seal it before stitching. Peel off the freezer paper and put aside to use again. Use a small round paintbrush and lightly dab the textile medium onto the coloured areas. Ensure you go right to the edges but do not get any onto the background fabric as it may stain. Do not 'push' the medium into the fabric as it may bleed your colour, simply 'sit' it on top and let it soak in. Leave to dry (only about ½ hour). Alternatively you can stitch your panel first and then seal afterwards. This makes the sealing process easier (you have a boundary for the medium) however the stitching process will take some intensity of colour from the panel.

Appliqué

Throughout the book the appliqué method used is fusible appliqué. You may choose to substitute your own preferred method, either needleturn, blind hem appliqué or the many other options available. Any method will work with the templates given.

For fusible appliqué trace the designs onto the paper side of your fusible webbing using a mechanical pencil. Cut out roughly around the drawn lines. Fuse the shapes to the wrong side of your chosen fabrics and cut out smoothly on the drawn lines. I use a good pair of paper

Tilly & friends

Quilt size approx 59 1/4" x 74 3/4"

See inside back cover for larger photo.

Requirements
40"/1m white stitchery fabric
45"/115cm assorted light pink fabrics
30"/80cm assorted dark pink fabrics
10"/25cm assorted light purples
10"/25cm assorted dark purples
35"/90cm assorted greens
15"/40cm green first border
22"/55cm outer border fabric
20"/50cm piping fabric
20"/50cm binding fabric
30"/80cm fusible pellon
40"/1m vliesofix fusible webbing
65"/165cm x 80"/2m backing
and batting
DMC threads and Derwent pencils as
per colour key.

Embellishments (Optional)
Hot fix crystals
Light rose - 11 x 3mm/10ss and
114 x 2mm/6ss

Alexandrite or Tanzanite -
43 x 3mm/10ss
Erinite - 33 x 2mm/6ss
Peridot - 10 x 3mm/10ss
Fuchsia - 28 x 3mm/10ss
and 78 x 2mm/6ss
Clear - 32 x 5mm/10ss
Fuchsia hearts -
51 x 6mm metallic
nailheads.

Cutting instructions - Centre quilt
From stitchery fabric cut:
For stitched blocks cut
nine squares 10" x 10"
- they will be trimmed
back to 8" x 8" after
stitching.

2 @ 4 1/2" x 10"	(D)
2 @ 3" x 6 1/2"	(G)
2 @ 3" x 7"	(H)
2 @ 7 1/2" x 3 1/2"	(M)
2 @ 5" x 3"	(O)
2 @ 3 1/2" x 6"	(S)
2 @ 4" x 6 1/2"	(V)

From assorted pinks cut:
18 strips 1 1/2" x 8"
18 strips 1 1/2" x 10"

From light pinks cut:

2 @ 5 1/2" x 10"	(A)
2 @ 4 1/2" x 5"	(C)
2 @ 3 1/2" x 6 1/2"	(F)
2 @ 5" x 10"	(J)
2 @ 4 1/2" x 10"	(L)
2 @ 5 1/2" x 3"	(P)
2 @ 7" x 6"	(R)
2 @ 3 1/2" x 10"	(T)
2 @ 3 1/2" x 6 1/2"	(W)

From dark pinks cut:
12 @ 1 1/2" x 10"
Four @ 11" x 11"

From light purples cut:

2 @ 5" x 6"	(B)
2 @ 6" x 4"	(E)
2 @ 3 1/2" x 3"	(I)
2 @ 3" x 10"	(K)
2 @ 3" x 3 1/2"	(N)
2 @ 4 1/2" x 10"	(Q)
2 @ 7" x 4"	(U)

From assorted greens cut:
64 squares 4" x 4"

First green border
From green fabric cut:
Two strips 2 7/8" x 50"
Two strips 2 7/8" x 55 1/4"

Pieced on point border
From white fabric cut:
Six squares 5" x 5"

From various green fabrics cut:
32 squares 2" x 2"

From dark purple squares cut:
40 squares 2" x 2"

From dark pinks cut:
28 strips 1" x 5"
28 strips 1" x 6"

From light pink fabrics cut:
Six squares 9" x 9" - cross cut twice
diagonally to give 24 quarter square
triangles

Four squares 4 3/4" x 4 3/4"- cross cut
once diagonally to give eight half
square triangles.

Outer border
From pink fabric cut: Seven strips
3" x width of fabric. Join using bias joins
into one long strip then cross cut
Two strips @ 59 3/4"
Two strips @ 70 1/4"

Piping
From stripe fabric cut:
1 1/4" wide strips on the true bias to
make approx 280" of piping.

Binding
From pink fabric cut: Seven strips 2 1/2"
x width of fabric. Join using bias joins
to make approx 280" of binding.

Tilly & friends

Preparation

If using an iron on transfer now is the time to transfer your design to the stitchery fabric. (the 9 fairy friends onto the stitchery fabric squares) Follow the instructions on your transfer sheet. Do a test piece using the transfer test included until you are satisfied with your iron settings and transfer result. If you are tracing you will need to locate the designs from pattern sheet #2. You may prefer to photocopy them onto separate sheets for ease of use. Use a light source such as a window or light box and a soft mechanical lead pencil to transfer carefully all designs ensuring they are centred on the fabric.

Colourqué™

Complete all colouring and sealing following the instructions on page 2 and the colour keys for each design. You may choose to change the colours to match your chosen fabrics. Use my colours as a guide only.

We will not attach the crystals until after construction of the quilt.

Stitchery

Lay the pellon behind your stitchery design and press with a hot steam iron until the pellon glue has melted and fused. Place it into a 6-8" embroidery hoop. Have the fabric firm but not stretched out of shape. Use a No. 7 or 8 crewel needle and 1-2 strands of DMC cotton thread to stitch all drawn lines following the stitch guide. Once the stitching is finished, press carefully. Seal now if you didn't do it before stitching. Trim your stitcheries carefully back to 8" x 8" ensuring you centre the designs. Press well.

Emmy Lou

Face, hands - 10 Hair - 9 Eyes, boots - 7 Wings - 3
Cheeks, bows (C) , Collar & frills (K), dress (B,C,D) - 11
Dress flowers, Dress bodice (F) - 13
36 x 2mm Fuchsia crystals 10 x 3mm Fuchsia crystals

Abbey Isabella

Face, arms, legs - 10 Hair, eyes - 7
Wings, dress (B,D,H) - 3
10 x 3mm Peridot crystals
6 x 2mm Erinite crystals
1 x 3mm Light rose crystal

Georgie Girl

Face, hands, feet - 10
Hair - 5   Eyes - 7
Wings, skirt (D), bows (D), bodice (D) - 2
Striped wing inserts and skirt (D,H) - 6
7 x 2mm Erinite crystals
20 x 6mm Fuchsia hearts

Indianna Zoe

Livvy May

Face, nose - 10
Hair - 5   Eyes - 7
Mouth, wing outline, wing flowers - 3
Dress (B,D,E,G), wing running stitch - 13
17 x 3mm Alexandrite crystals
44 x 2mm Light rose crystals

Miss Molly Dolly

Hair - 9
Face, nose, eyes, hands - 10
Mouth, wings (B), shoes,
pink running stitch (B) - 3
Dress, dots, collar - 13(F)
38 x 2mm Light rose crystals
8 x 3mm
Fuchsia crystals

Tessie Bessie

Face, nose, legs - 10   Hair, eyes - 8

Mouth, Wings, dress skirt (B),
hem vertical stripes (D,F) - 11

Check dress bodice (D,F),
hem horizontal stripes (F) - 13

20 x 3mm Alexandrite crystals
10 x 6mm Fuchsia hearts

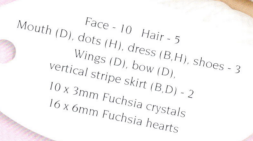

Face - 10   Hair - 5
Mouth (D), dots (H), dress (B,H), shoes - 3
Wings (D), bow (D),
vertical stripe skirt (B,D) - 2
10 x 3mm Fuchsia crystals
16 x 6mm Fuchsia hearts

Sarah Rose

Face, arms, feet - 10 Hair, eyes - 7
Collar (I), dress (I), dress bodice (D), shoes (D) - 2
Wings - 3
42 x 2mm Fuchsia crystal
5 x 3mm Light rose crystals

Construction

Note that all seams are ¼" unless otherwise stated

- Lay out your stitched blocks in the chosen order and lay assorted pink strips around all edges taking care to distribute the strips evenly over the quilt top.

- Attach an 8" pink strip to the top and bottom of all stitchery blocks. Press towards the pink.

- Attach a 10" pink strip to the sides of each block. Press towards the pink.

- Draw a diagonal pencil line using your mechanical pencil and a sheet of sandpaper to stabilise across the back of all green 4" squares.

- Layout your blocks as before and now position your assorted green squares on every corner again with even distribution of colours across the quilt.

- Lay a green square right sides together on a corner of your stitchery block. Stitch on the drawn line and press the triangle back towards the point of your block taking care not to distort the bias line. Carefully trim away the middle green layer of fabric to reduce bulk.

- Repeat for all green squares.

- Join your stitchery blocks, firstly in three rows of three, and then join the rows together pinning and matching all of the green triangle seams.

Borders:

- Follow the piecing guide below to join all marked pieces to make the first border blocks.

Top Appliqué Border

Left Side Border

Right Side Border

Bottom Appliqué Border

- Attach the pink strips to the sides as shown and press seams towards the pink.

- You will then need to attach your green squares to the designated corners as shown. Trim middle layer as before.

- Join the border blocks together and attach a large square to the ends of the top and bottom border.

Left Side Border

Right Side Border

Top Appliqué Border

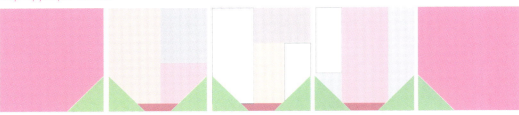

Bottom Appliqué Border

Flower A **Flower B** **Flower C** **Flower D**

Flower E **Flower F** **Leaf G** **Leaf H**

Appliqué

Top and bottom borders:

Use the Tilly and Friends appliqué templates on the design sheet #1 to trace the designs onto the paper side of your vliesofix fusible webbing. See page 2 for more detailed instructions for appliquéing.

Side borders:

Use the Tilly and Friends side border appliqué design on Design sheet #1. Trace all shapes twice, one for each side.

Fuse the shapes to the wrong side of your various fabric scraps. Use the photographs as guides for colour choice. Cut out smoothly on the drawn lines. When positioning have vines flowing in opposite directions either side. (mirrored).

Stems - make yourself approx 3.5m/4yds of ¼" bias strips using your preferred method. (see page 3 for ideas).

Again using the diagram and photograph remove the paper backing from your appliqué shapes and position over the top and bottom border strips until you are happy. Tuck the ends of the stems under the flowers and let them hang over the raw edges of the borders. Fuse to secure with your hot dry iron. (keep aside the flowers for the green squares)

Use 1 strand of matching Stranded cotton and a fine #7/8 Crewel or Applibond needle to stitch around all raw edges with a buttonhole stitch. You may choose to do this step by machine if you have a buttonhole stitch function or you could use a satin stitch.

Now attach the side borders to your quilt top pressing seams towards the centre. Then attach the top and bottom matching the seams at each corner. Again press to the centre. This secures the ends of the stems into the seam.

You can now fuse the flowers to the green squares and complete the buttonhole stitching as before.

Green border - fold your top and bottom border strips in half and half again. Mark each fold with a pin. Do the same on the top and bottom of your quilt. Pin the border strips right sides together matching all pin markings. Stitch and press seams towards green border strips. Repeat with side borders.

On point pieced border:

- Join green and dark purple 2″ squares together to form 8 nine patch blocks. Press all seams towards purple so that they are mirrored when joining strips.

- Attach dark pink 5″ strips to two sides of each block. Press to pink. Do the same with your white squares.

- Attach 6″ strips to the remaining two sides of all of these blocks. Again press to the pink.

Use your light box to trace the designs onto all white squares. Follow the colour and design guides and the photograph to Colourqué™ your blocks as before. Place each one into an embroidery hoop and stitch. Seal now if you chose this option.

Flower B
Centre - B, D ,11
Outer petals - D, 11
Inner petals - E,G, 1
Crystals clear x 12

Flower A
Centre - E,G, 1
Outer petals -E, 1
Inner petals - B,G, 4
Crystals clear x 5

Face, arms, feet - 10   Hair - 8
Bows (G), skirt (B,G,H) - 11
Dress bodice (B), shoes (B),
skirt vertical stripes (B,H) - 4
Mouth, heart (C) - 11
32x2mm Fuchsia crystals
5x3mm Light rose crystals
5x6mm Fuchsia heart nailheads

Tilly May

- Layout your nine patch and Colourqué'd blocks as per the photograph with the light pink triangles in between.

- Join each border strip in diagonal rows, then pin match the seams and join each diagonal piece together to make the full border row.

- Fold border strips in half and half again, place a pin at each fold. Repeat with the top and bottom of your quilt. Match the pin marks and attach the top and bottom borders. Press seams to green border strip. Ensure you have the top border up the correct way.

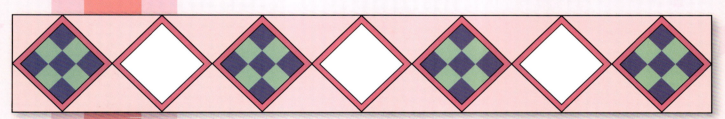

Final border

Halve and quarter your border strips and quilt top as before. Attach the top and bottom first and then the two side borders pressing towards the pink border to finish.

Quilting

If you are having your quilt professionally quilted now is the time to pack it up and send it off!

If doing it yourself read on…

Layer your quilt following the guidelines on page 3.

You can now quilt your quilt as you desire or as I have done.

With a walking foot quilt in the ditch of all straight borders. Next quilt in the ditch down both sides of the pink strips between the blocks and around the outside of each green pieced square.

Ditch on the inside and outside of the pink border strips in the top and bottom on point borders.

Straight stitch some lines inside the green border. I used the edge of my walking foot as a guide and stitched double lines either side of the green strips.

Now change to a free machine or darning foot and drop your feed dogs.

Outline all appliqué and Colourqué™ designs. Do a small filler (I used a loopy design) behind the nine Fairy designs and the Colourque'd blocks in the top and bottom on point borders.

Echo quilt 3 times around the vertical floral vines in the side borders.

Free machine quilt a flower shape in each nine patch block to match an appliquéd flower and in each light pink triangle (half flowers and quarter flowers in the sides and corners) on the top and bottom on point border.

Quilt a large stipple or meander in the outside pink border.

Piping

I have given basic instructions for piping, however I recommend the 'Piping hot Binding' tool and book for very extensive never fail instructions. www.PiecesBeWithYou.com

Steam or prewash your 280" of piping cord to shrink it well.

Join your bias strips and press seams open. Press in half wrong sides together along the length.

Lay the cord inside the fold of the bias strip and push right into the fold. Use a zipper, piping or cording foot to stitch as close as possible to the cord without catching it. You may be able to adjust your needle position to perfect this.

Trim the edges of your piping back to $\frac{1}{4}$" from the stitching line as evenly as possible.

Attach the piping to the quilt top doing one side at a time. Have the raw edges even (the piped edge is towards the centre of the quilt) and stitch directly over the previous stitching line. Repeat for each side of the quilt.

Binding and finishing

Fold and press binding strips wrong sides together along the length.

Leaving a 10" tail begin pinning the binding to the top side of the quilt half way along one side. Turn the quilt over and stitch from the back one thread to the left of the previous stitching line (the one which attached the piping). Stitch to the intersection of stitching lines at the corner and backstitch. Turn the quilt over and fold binding down away from the quilt (you will have a 45° fold) then back up again in the new direction. Pin along this side. Turn to the back and begin stitching again one thread to the left. Repeat this around your quilt. When you get to the last side stop approximately 15" from your starting point. Measure, cut and join your two ends using a 45° join. Finger press the seam and complete the stitching again from the back. Trim any excess batting and backing fabric to $\frac{1}{2}$" from the stitching line.

Clip corners and turn binding to the back of the quilt.Pin and slip stitch using a matching thread to the binding. Fold and stitch the mitred corners neatly on the front and back.

Now you can attach your crystals or other embellishments if you wish. Use the photographs and colour guides for placement.

Last but not least, add a label to your quilt. Maybe you can design your own Colourque'd label using the design elements from the front of the quilt.

fairy floss

Quilt size approx 58" x 72"

Requirements

Various pink fabrics - total of 24" /60cm

Various green fabrics - total of 24" /60cm

White stitchery fabric - with no joins 56"(1 2/3 yds) /1.4m

Pink border fabric - with no joins 73" (2 1/8yds) / 1.85m

- with joins - 57"(1 1/2/3yds) /1.45m

Binding fabric - bias binding - 29"/75cm

Backing fabric/batting - 62" x 76"/2m x 1.5m

DMC Stranded cottons -155, 604, 961, and 3013

Derwent pencils - 1800, 2000, 2100, 2500, 2700, 4800, 5100

100% cotton cream sewing thread

Matching quilting threads

Embellishments (optional)

40 x 3mm/10ss hot fix Light rose crystals

64 x 5mm/20ss clear hot fix crystals

Instructions

Cutting Instructions

From pink fabrics cut:
14 squares $7\frac{1}{4}$" x $7\frac{1}{4}$"

From pink border fabric cut:
Six strips $1\frac{1}{2}$" x $54\frac{1}{2}$"
Two strips $9\frac{1}{2}$" x $72\frac{1}{2}$" (you may wish to
check measure these across your quilt before cutting)
Two strips $9\frac{1}{2}$" x $40\frac{1}{2}$" (you may wish to
check measure these across your quilt before cutting)

From green fabrics cut:
54 squares $3\frac{7}{8}$" x $3\frac{7}{8}$"

From white stitchery fabric cut:
Two strips 10" x 56"

From stripe binding fabric cut:
Strips on the true bias 2" wide. Join to make approximately
300" of binding.

Preparation

Using a sheet of sandpaper to stabilise and a mechanical
pencil draw a diagonal line on the back of all green squares.

Using a light box or window light source and a soft
mechanical lead pencil trace the stitchery design from
Design sheet#1 onto both white strips of fabric. You will
need to fold the strips to find the centre and place the
centre of the design at this point. Trace one end and then
flip the design for the other end.

Colourqué™ and stitchery

Following the instructions on page 2 and the colour
guide colour all of your vines, leaves and flowers. You
can either seal the colour now with your textile medium
or after stitching as I did. Place your strips into a 6-8"
embroidery hoop and begin stitching using two strands of
DMC cotton thread and a NO7/8 crewel needle as per the
colour guide. When finished press well and trim the strips
back to $8\frac{1}{2}$" x $54\frac{1}{2}$" ensuring the designs are centred.

Flower A
Centre - E,G, 1
Outer petals -E, 1
Inner petals - B,G, 4
Crystals clear x 5

Flower B
Centre - B, D ,11
Outer petals - D, 11
Inner petals - E,G, 1
Crystals clear x 12

Circle flowers D
B, C, 4
Light rose crystals -3
on small flowers,
7 on large

Leaves and vine
K, L, - 12

fairy floss cont.

Construction - Note that all seams are ¼" unless otherwise stated.

Using 14 x 7¼" pink squares and 54 x 3⅞" green squares, we will be making flying geese units.

Place two of the green squares right sides together on opposite sides of a pink large square. Sew a scant ¼" either side of the drawn line. Trim the corners as per the diagram to keep your work neat and easier to piece together later.

 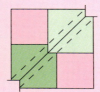

Next place another green square right sides together over the corner of the large pink triangle. Sew a scant ¼" seam on either side. Cut apart on the drawn line and press the seam allowance towards the smaller triangle again. Repeat for the remaining units.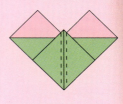

You should now have 54 flying geese units measuring 3½" x 6½".

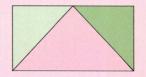 

Lay out your geese in three strips of 18 arranging the colours evenly throughout the strips. When joining your strips have the point stitching junction uppermost so that you can ensure you intersect the seam junction perfectly.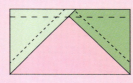

Press all seams in one direction with the bulk away from the points.

Fold each strip in half and half again and place a pin at each fold mark.

Do the same with your six 1½" x 54½" pink strips.

Attach a pink strip to either side of each geese strip by matching the pin marks, pinning and stitching. Press to pink strips.

Join your three geese strips and two stitchery strips as per the photograph. Use the fold and pin match method to join all strips so that they sit evenly. Press all seams towards the thin pink border strips.

Check measure across your quilt top and complete the cutting of your border strips. Join the top and bottom border strips again using the fold and pin match method and finally attach your side borders.

Trim all threads from behind the white stitchery strips so they do not show through after quilting.

Quilting

If you are having your quilt professionally quilted now is the time to pack it up and send it off!

If doing it yourself read on…

Layer your quilt following the guidelines on page 3.

You can now quilt your quilt as you desire or as I have done. With a walking foot quilt in the ditch either side of the white stitchery strips and around the ditch of the outer border.

Now change to a free machine or darning foot and drop your feed dogs.

Outline all Colourqué™ designs in the white strips. Do a filler (I used a loopy design) behind the floral vines.

Either free machine a $\frac{1}{4}$" inside each goose block using a matching pink thread or change back to your walking foot to get a more even stitch.

Scallop border

Make a template of each scallop design from your design sheet. Use a blue water erasable pen or chalk pencil and mark each corner template (A) on your outer border. (the templates should lie $\frac{1}{4}$" inside the outer raw edge of the borders)

Fold the short sides in half to get the centre mark (this should match with the centre of your flying geese strip) and place the smaller scallop (B) matching the centre mark. Trace the outline.

Now use the C template to trace either side of the centre one and evenly down the long sides. If your measurements are not exact just adjust slightly as you go stretching or reducing the width of the scallops to fit. You may wish to find the centre point of the long sides also and work from the centre outwards.

Back to quilting

Using your walking foot quilt on the drawn scallop line around the outside edge of your quilt. I then echoed two rows inside of this line using the edge of my walking foot and changing the needle position to the left to get an even distance.

Change to your darning foot and drop those feed dogs again. Complete by repeating your filler design (large loopys for me) in the remainder of the border.

Binding and finishing

Fold and press binding strips wrong sides together along the length.

Leaving a 6" tail begin attaching the binding to the top side of the quilt half way around one scallop. Stitch to the inner point, with needle down, lift the foot, turn quilt and fold and tuck the binding in using a pin to help get it in the new direction.

Take care not to stretch the bias binding around the curves. Repeat this around your quilt. When you get to the last side stop as soon as you get around a point. Measure, cut and join your two ends using a 45° join. Finger press the seam and complete the stitching again to the end.

Clip corners and turn binding to the back of the quilt. Pin and slip stitch using a matching thread to the binding. Fold and stitch the mitred corners neatly on the front and back.

Now you can attach your crystals or other embellishments if you wish. Use the photograph and colour guides for placement.

Don't forget to add your label to the quilt. Why not make a Colourqué™ label up using the design from the front of the quilt.

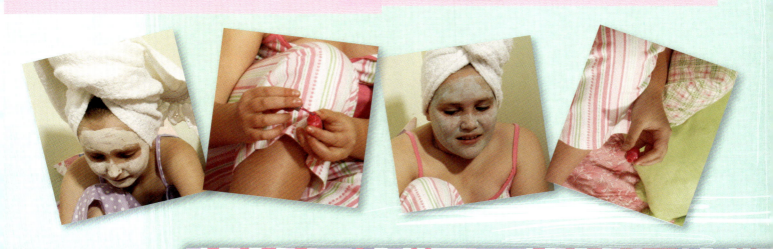

popcorn

Quilt size approx 52¹/₂" x 44¹/₂"

This quilt uses 60° diamonds. You do not need to have a special ruler for this but it may assist. Many standard 6¹/₂" x 24" rulers have a 60° line on them or you can make yourself a template.

Requirements

Various light purple fabrics-24"/60cm
Various green fabrics - 24"/60cm
White stitchery fabric - no joins 55"/ 1.4m / with joins 30" / 75cm
1st border and binding fabric - 22" / 55cm
2nd border fabric - no joins 53" / 1.35m / with joins 39"/1m
Backing and batting - 56" x 60" / 1.4m x 1.5m
DMC Stranded threads - 155, 604, 3013
Derwent pencils - 1800, 2000, 2500, 2700, 4800, 5100
100% cotton sewing thread
Matching quilting threads
Embellishments (optional)
144 x 3mm/10ss Light Rose hot fix crystals
100 x 3mm/10ss Light amethyst hot fix crystals

Cutting instructions

From light purple fabrics cut:
Nine purple diamonds $6\frac{1}{2}$" x $6\frac{1}{2}$"

From light green fabrics cut:
Four diamonds $6\frac{1}{2}$" x $6\frac{1}{2}$"

To rotary cut the diamonds first cut a strip on the straight grain $6\frac{1}{2}$" wide by approx $11\frac{1}{2}$" for each diamond. (you may want to cut 2 of each colour from a strip approx $6\frac{1}{2}$" x $21\frac{1}{2}$"). Place the 60 ° line on the edge of the strip and cut the corner off diagonally.

$6\frac{1}{2}$" x $11\frac{1}{2}$"

cut here

60" line on ruler

Now measure $6\frac{1}{2}$" along from this cut and cut again in the same diagonal direction.

cut here

From light green fabrics cut:
Four diamonds $7\frac{1}{2}$" x $7\frac{1}{2}$"
One diamond $8\frac{1}{2}$" x $8\frac{1}{2}$"

Follow the same directions above but cut your strips wider to the given width.

Cross cut two of the $7\frac{1}{2}$" diamonds vertically and two horizontally for side units.

Cross cut the $8\frac{1}{2}$" in both directions for corner units.

From white stitchery fabric cut:
Eighteen rectangular diamonds $6\frac{1}{2}$" x 3" (cut 3" strips across width of fabric and cross cut 60° angles again using your ruler or template. Make sure all of the angles are going in the same direction as your diamonds.

Cut two strips 55" x 3" (as this is a sashing strip it is preferable not to have a join if you can help it)
Cut two strips 35" x 3"
Cut two strips 15" x 3"

From dark purple fabric (first border) cut: (you may wish to check measure these across your quilt before cutting).

Two strips $1\frac{1}{4}$ " x 51"
Two strips $1\frac{1}{4}$" x $32\frac{1}{2}$"

From minkee blankee or light purple fabric (2nd border) cut: you may wish to check measure these across your quilt before cutting)

Two strips $6\frac{1}{2}$" x 53"
Two strips $6\frac{1}{2}$" x 45"

Construction

Layout all your diamonds, side units and corner units as per the photograph.

Attach a $6\frac{1}{2}''$ white diamond strip to one side of every diamond. Join together in rows and complete each row with a white strip on the end.

Carefully attach the side pieces ensuring you take care with bias seams.

Attach corner units to both ends of your longest centre diagonal strip.

Press all seams away from white.

Now use your long sashing strips to join your rows together taking care to match the rows across the sashing strip so that they line up evenly. Press away from the white fabric. Finally attach the remaining two corner units.

Lay your ruler along the sides and trim back excess side and corner units to within $\frac{1}{4}''$ of the stitching junctions of each seam. Take care to square the quilt particularly at the corners by using the lines on your ruler to get square edges.

Stitchery

Using the design on sheet #2, a light box or window light source and a soft mechanical lead pencil trace the vine repeat in every sashing strip. Adjust the design slightly to fit if necessary as you go. Follow the photograph for guidance.

Colourque™

Following the instructions on page 2 and the colour guide colour all of your vines, leaves and flowers. Seal the colour with your textile medium and then place your top into a 6-8" embroidery hoop and begin stitching using one strand of DMC cotton thread and a NO7/8 crewel needle as per the colour guide. When finished press well and trim all threads from the back of your quilt so that they do not show through the white sashing strips.

Flower centre - B,C,4
Outer petals - C,4
Inner petals - E,G,1
Crystals - 3mm Light amethyst x 5

Leaves - K,L, 12
Vines - 12 stem stitch

Circle flowers - Light rose B,C,4
Crystals - Light rose 3mm x1

Finishing

1st border:

Check measure across the centre of your top in both directions and complete the cutting of your border strips.

Fold your top in half and half again along the length and mark each fold with a pin. Repeat this with the two longer dark purple strips. Match the pin marks and attach the border strips to the quilt top ensuring the stitching line passes through the previous stitch junctions to get nice points.

Repeat this procedure with the top and bottom borders.

2nd border:

Again check measure and complete cutting of your border strips.

Repeat the above steps to attach firstly the side borders and then the top and bottom borders as before. If using Minkee blankee which can be quite slippery it may be best to have the minkee on the underside of the top or use a walking foot or dual feed to assist.

Quilting

Using a matching thread and walking foot I quilted in the ditch of all white sashing strips.

Next I quilted in the ditch around the inner narrow border and stitched a basting stitch around the outside edge of the quilt.

I then changed to a free machine foot, dropped my feed dogs and did a large meander in each diamond and half diamond area. Because I used a soft Minkee spot fabric for my border I did not do any further quilting in this area. If you used a standard border fabric and a batting you may wish to quilt a design in the outer border. As the feature of this quilt is the vine stitchery in the sashing strips I kept the quilting to a minimum so as not to deter from the stitchery.

Binding and finishing

Fold and press binding strips wrong sides together along the length.

Leaving a 6" tail begin attaching the binding to one side of the quilt. Continue around the quilt mitring the corners as you go. Stop approximately 10" from your starting point. Measure, cut and join your two ends using a 45° join. Finger press the seam and complete the stitching again to the end.

Clip corners and turn binding to the back of the quilt. Pin and slip stitch using a matching thread to the binding. Fold and stitch the mitred corners neatly on the front and back.

Now you can attach your crystals or any other embellishments if you wish. Use the photograph and colour guides for placement.

Again don't forget to add your label to the quilt. Why not make another Colourquéd label using the design elements from the front of the quilt.

cupcake wallhanging

Requirements

15"/40cm square of white stitchery fabric
15"/40cm fusible pellon
DMC Threads: 604, 838, 841, 961,
Derwent pencils: 1800, 2000, 2700, 4400
Textile Medium

Embellishments (optional)

32 x 2mm Light rose crystal
8 x 3mm Light rose crystals
5 x 5mm/20ss clear crystals
5 x Fuchsia heart nailheads

Preparation

If using an iron on transfer now is the time to transfer your design to the stitchery fabric. Follow the instructions on your transfer sheet. Do a test piece using the transfer test included until you are satisfied with your iron settings and transfer result. If you are tracing you will need to locate the design from pattern sheet #2. You may prefer to photocopy it onto a separate sheet for ease of use. Use a light source such as a window or light box and a soft mechanical lead pencil to transfer carefully all designs ensuring they are centred on the fabric.

Colourqué™

Complete all colouring and sealing following the instructions on page 2 and the colour key on the next page. You may choose to change the colours to match your chosen fabrics. Use my colours as a guide only.

We will not attach the crystals until after all stitching and sealing is complete.

Stitchery

Lay the pellon behind your stitchery design and press with a hot steam iron until the pellon glue has melted and fused. Place it into a 6-8" embroidery hoop. Have the fabric firm but not stretched out of shape. Use a No. 7 or 8 crewel needle and 1-2 strands of DMC cotton thread to stitch all drawn lines following the stitch guide. Once the stitching is finished, press carefully. Seal now if you didn't do it before stitching. Press well.

Now you can attach your crystals or any other embellishments if you wish. Use the photograph and colour guides for placement.

Your stitchery is now ready to frame or to use in your own preferred project.

tilly may

Face, arms, feet - 10

Hair - 8

Bows (G), skirt (B,G,H) - 11

Dress bodice (B), shoes (B),
skirt vertical stripes (B,H) - 4

Mouth, heart (C) - 11

Crystals - Light rose 3mm x 8,
Light rose 2mm x 32, Fuchsia hearts x 5

Flower A: Centre - E,G, 1, Outer petals - E, 1
Inner petals - B,G, 4

Crystals, clear x 5
Leaves and vine - K,L, - 12

the tilly dilly bag

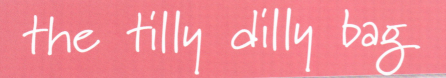

Requirements

2½"/5cm white fabric
2½"/5cm scraps pinks and greens
32"/80cm lining fabric
5"/13cm scraps for flowers
5"/13cm fusible pellon
4"/10cm Steam a Seam® iron on fusible web
DMC Stranded thread 603
3 x 1½"/3cm buttons

Cutting instructions

From white fabric cut: One strip 2½" x 31"
From various pink and
green fabrics cut:
seven strips 2½" x 31"
From Lining fabric cut:
one piece 31" x 27"

construction

- Sew all strips together placing a white strip in the centre. Press seams in one direction.
- Hand stitch a running stitch using 2 strands of DMC thread along the centre white strip ⅛" from both edges.
- Join the large lining piece to the stripped section along the top edge.
- Fold right sides together and stitch down the long side matching seams and leaving a 1" opening in the lining just above the seam where it joins the stripped piece.
- Turn the bag so that the seam is in the centre back. Stitch across the bottom edge and the top of the lining edge leaving a 3" opening for turning.

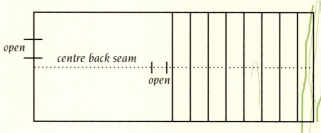

open

centre back seam

open

Construction cont.

- Clip corners and turn bag through to right side. Slip stitch top opening closed.

- Push lining down into bag, forcing the corners into the corners of the bag. Press.

- Stitch a row of stitching in the ditch between the stripped piece and the lining and again 1" above this to form a casing.

- Thread your cord through the opening in the casing strip and tie ends.

- Flowers - make a template of appliqué flower A from the pattern sheet#1.

- Trace 3 flowers onto the wrong side of your flower fabric.

- Fuse pellon to wrong side of another piece of your flower fabric.

- Lay the two pieces together and using a small stitch length stitch on the drawn line.

- Trim the seam back to 1/8", clip into the points and around the curves.

- Make a slit in the non pellon side and turn the flower through. Press well ensuring you make nice curved petals.

- Using two strands of DMC thread stitch a blanket stitch around the outside edges of the petals.

- Using your inner petal fabric and a light box trace 3 inner petal A shapes onto the right side of your fabric with a soft lead pencil or washout marker. Fuse this fabric to one side of the steam a seam webbing and a backing fabric to the other. Cut out just inside the drawn line so that none of your markings are showing. Position inner petals on your outer petal shapes.

Attach your 3D flowers down the centre of the dilly bag with a large button.

doona cover

Requirements

62"/1.55m of 92"/2.3m wide white sateen, cotton or sheeting fabric.

76"/1.9m of 92"/2.3m or wider pink backing fabric.

8"/20cm various greens. 8"/20cm various purples.

8"/20cm piping fabric.

Scraps of various pinks, greens, purples for appliqué.

20"/½ m of vliesofix fusible webbing.

70"/1.75m piping cord.

DMC Threads 155,604,772

For a single size doona approx 60" x 88"

Cutting instructions

From white cotton sateen fabric cut:
One piece 62½" x 60½"
One piece 20½" x 60½"

From pink backing fabric cut:
One piece 60½" x 88½"
One piece 60½" x 15½"

From green fabrics cut:
45 squares 2½" OR
3 strips 2½" x width of fabric

From purple fabrics cut:
45 squares 2½" OR
3 strips 2½" x width of fabric

From stripe fabric cut:
1¼" wide true bias strips - join to make 65".

Appliqué

Use the Tilly and Friends appliqué templates on the design sheet #1 to trace the designs onto the paper side of your vliesofix fusible webbing. You will need: 3 x flower A, 2 x flower B, 1 x flower C, 5 x flower D, 2 x flower E, 2 x flower F, 10 x leaf H and 12 x leaf G. Cut out roughly.

Fuse the shapes to the wrong side of your various fabric scraps. Use the photographs as guides for colour choice. Cut out smoothly on the drawn lines.

Stems - make yourself approx 1m/1¼yd of ¼" binding strips using your preferred method. (see page 3 for ideas).

Again using the diagram and photograph remove the paper backing from your appliqué shapes and position along the bottom edge of the 62½" x 60½" piece of sateen (the shorter side) until you are happy. Tuck the ends of the stems under the flowers and let them hang over the raw edge of the fabric. Fuse to secure with your hot dry iron. Stitch using 1-2 strands of DMC threads or by machine if you have a buttonhole or satin stitch.

Construction

Join green and purple strips together to make 6 strips of green/purple/green and 3 strips of purple/green/purple. Press all strips towards the purple.

Cross cut 2½" strips and join alternately to make a strip 6½" x 60½" wide.

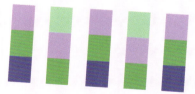

Join this strip to the bottom edge of your appliquéd sateen. The seam will secure the bottom of your stems.

Attach the piping along the bottom edge of your pieced strip.

Attach the 20½" piece of sateen on top of your piping and pieced strip ensuring the stitching line is one thread to the left of the previous stitching line. (have the pieced strip to the top so that you can see the piping stitch line)

Double fold a ½ "seam on one 60½" end of both pink pieces of backing fabric. Edge stitch.

Lay the large piece right sides together over the top of your doona top. Have the top raw edges even which will make the bottom hemmed edge lay just short of the top. Lay the short pink piece right sides together and raw edges even at the bottom of your doona top. It will be sitting over the larger pink piece by approx 13-14" and will form an envelope sleeve.

Stitch around all edges and neaten seams. Trim corners and turn the doona cover through to the right side. Press well and insert your doona....

Use these ideas to make matching curtains for your window. Measure the width of your window and multiply it by 2. As the chequerboard blocks are 2" finished, round up or down your measurement so it is divisible by 2 to enable easy piecing. Eg window width 125cm. Cut two drops at 124cm width (plus seam allowances). You would then make two pieced chequerboard strips 62 blocks wide. Attach the pieced strip to the bottom edge of your curtains. You may then attach another plain strip to the bottom to hem your curtains. Use the flower theme to add a valance or header treatment to the top.

pillowcase

Requirements

Total 3"/10cm various green fabrics

Total of 3"/10cm various purple fabrics

50"/1.3m white sateen, cotton or sheeting
fabric (44"/112cm wide) or
25"/65cm of (92"/2.3m wide) fabric

One strip of Green fabric for vines

20"/50cm strip of piping fabric

25"/65cm piping cord

5"/13cm scraps for flowers

Vliesofix fusible webbing paper

Green, pink and purple fabric scraps

DMC Threads 155, 604, 772

Cutting instructions

From green fabrics cut:12 squares $2\frac{1}{2}$" x $2\frac{1}{2}$"

From purple fabrics cut:12 squares $2\frac{1}{2}$" x $2\frac{1}{2}$"

From white fabric cut:
One strip $5\frac{1}{2}$" x $24\frac{1}{2}$"
One strip $2\frac{1}{2}$" x $24\frac{1}{2}$"
One piece $24\frac{1}{2}$" x $34\frac{1}{2}$"
One piece $24\frac{1}{2}$" x $32\frac{1}{2}$"

From stripe piping fabric cut:
On true bias one strip $1\frac{1}{4}$" x 25"

Appliqué

Following the appliqué instructions on page 2 trace one of flower A, two of flower D, Leaf G and leaf H from design sheet #1. Make two vine bias strips as you have done previously and position following the photograph and diagram on the white $5\frac{1}{2}$" strip of fabric.

Use one strand of DMC stranded thread to blanket stitch all edges following the photograph for colour placement.

Construction

Note all seams are $1/4$" unless otherwise stated

- Join green and purple squares alternately to make two strips of 12 squares.
- Attach one pieced strip to ether side of your appliquéd strip. Press to pieced strips.

- Make piping as per instructions on page 15 and sew to edge of one pieced strip.
- Lay $24\frac{1}{2}$" x $34\frac{1}{2}$" piece of white fabric right sides together with the piped edge. Have the stitching line from your piping on the top so that you can now stitch through all layers one thread to the left of this line. Press to piping.

Attach the $2\frac{1}{2}$" white strip to the other green/purple pieced strip. This is your pillow case top.

2"

Double Fold and press a 1" hem on the right hand end of the top. Edge stitch. Double fold a 1" hem on one end of your large backing piece. Edge stitch.

Lay the top and backing right sides together with the left ends even. (pieced end of top and non hemmed end of back)

The top piece will overhang the backing by approx 13". Mark with a pin 2" from the backing end and then fold the rest of the top from this point to the back sandwiching the backing piece in between. Stitch around the three open sides of the pillow case.

Clip corners and turn pillowcase right side out. Press well. Stitch a row of stitching 2" inside the outside edge on all sides. Insert pillow.

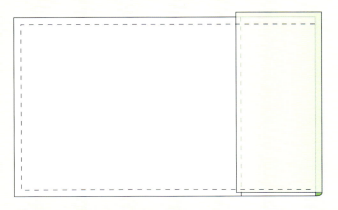

Notes

If you have chosen your own thread and pencil colours to match your fabrics, jot down your personal colour key here to refer to whilst making your projects.

DMC Stranded cottons

1. 155 - Forget me knot blue
2. 601 - Dark cranberry
3. 603 - Cranberry
4. 604 - Light cranberry
5. 729 - Medium old gold
6. 772 - Very light yellow green
7. 801 - Dark coffee brown
8. 838 - Very dark beige brown
9. 840 - Medium beige brown
10. 841 - Light beige brown
11. 961 - Dark rusty rose
12. 3013 - Light khaki green
13. 3746 - Dark blue violet

**Derwent colour pencils -
Artist or studio pencil range**

A. 0500 - Straw yellow
B. 1800 - Rose Pink
C. 2000 - Crimson Lake
D. 2100 - Rose madder lake
E. 2500 - Dark violet
F. 2600 - Light violet
G. 2700 - Blue violet lake
H. 4400 - Water green
I. 4500 - Mineral green
J. 4600 - Emerald green
K. 4800 - May green
L. 5100 - Olive Green

Tilly and Friends
Side border appliqué design
Trace two of each on paper
side of fusible webbing.

C

Pyjama Party Design Sheet #1

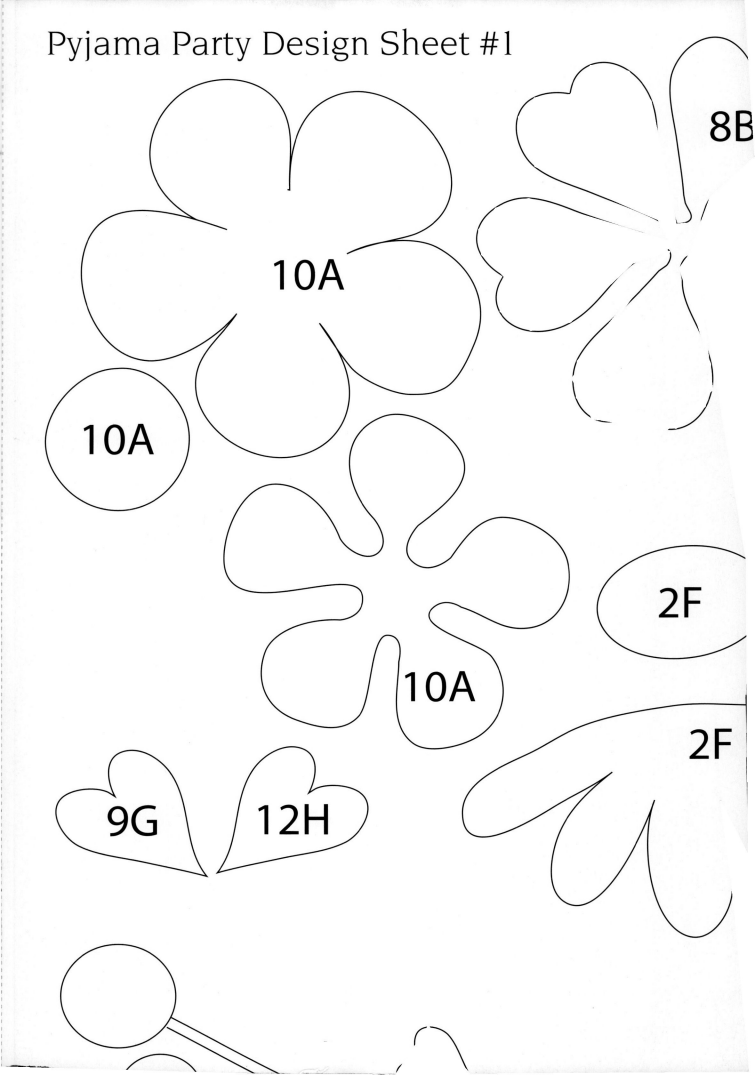

10A

8B

10A

10A

2F

2F

9G   12H

Fairy Floss
Scallop Template C - sides
Position straight edge on seam line.

C

ded cottons
orget me knot blue
Dark cranberry
ranberry
ight cranberry
edium old gold
ery light yellow green
Dark coffee brown
Very dark beige brown
Medium beige brown
Light beige brown
Dark rusty rose
Light khaki green
Dark blue violet

lour pencils –
udio pencil range

Straw yellow
Rose Pink
Crimson Lake
Rose madder lake
Dark violet
Light violet
Blue violet lake
Water green
Mineral green
Emerald green
May green
Olive green

Fairy Floss
Scallop template B
Position at centre of short sides
with straight edge on seam.

C

Tilly and Friends Quilt

Applique shapes -
Trace onto paper side
of fusible webbing as
per quantities given.

6C

6C

Colour

DMC St

1.   155
2.   601
3.   603
4.   604
5.   729
6.   772
7.   801
8.   838
9.   840
10. 841
11. 961
12. 301
13. 374

Derwen
Artist or

A.   050
B.   180
C.   200
D.   210
E.   250
F.   260
G.   270
H.   440
I.   450
J.   460
K.   480
L.   510

Fairy Floss
Scallop Template A - Corner
Position corner point
on seam junction.

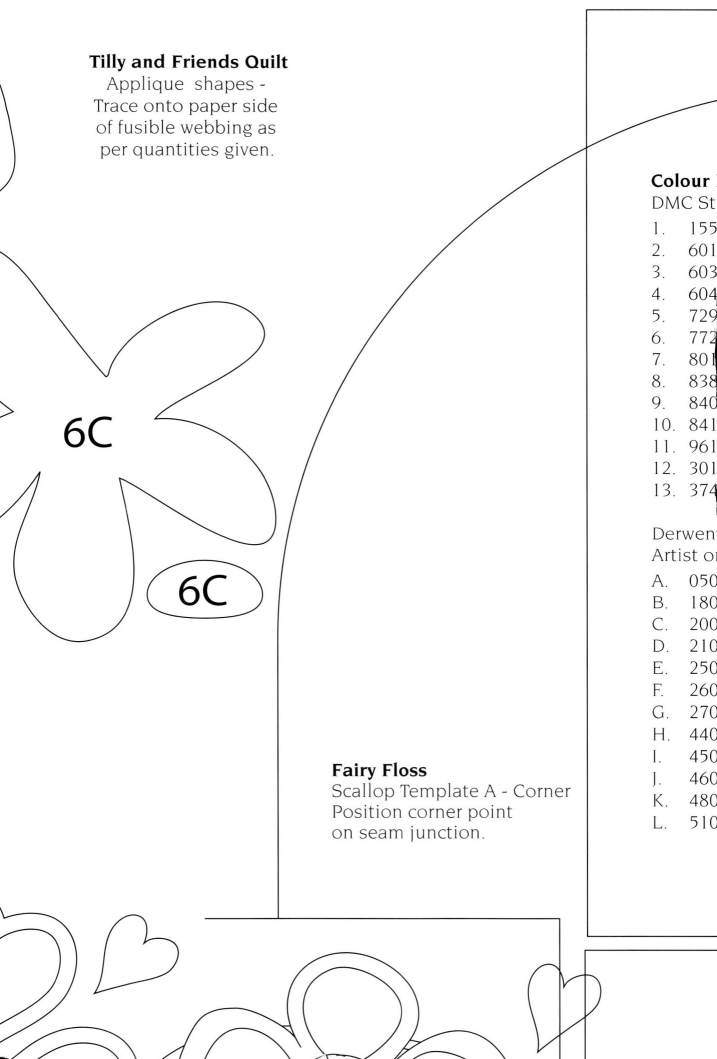

Pyjama Party Design Sheet #2

Flower B on-point border
Tilly and Friends quilt

ly May - Centre block
- point border
ly and Friends quilt

Sashing Stitchery Design
'Popcorn' quilt

Cu
Wa
De

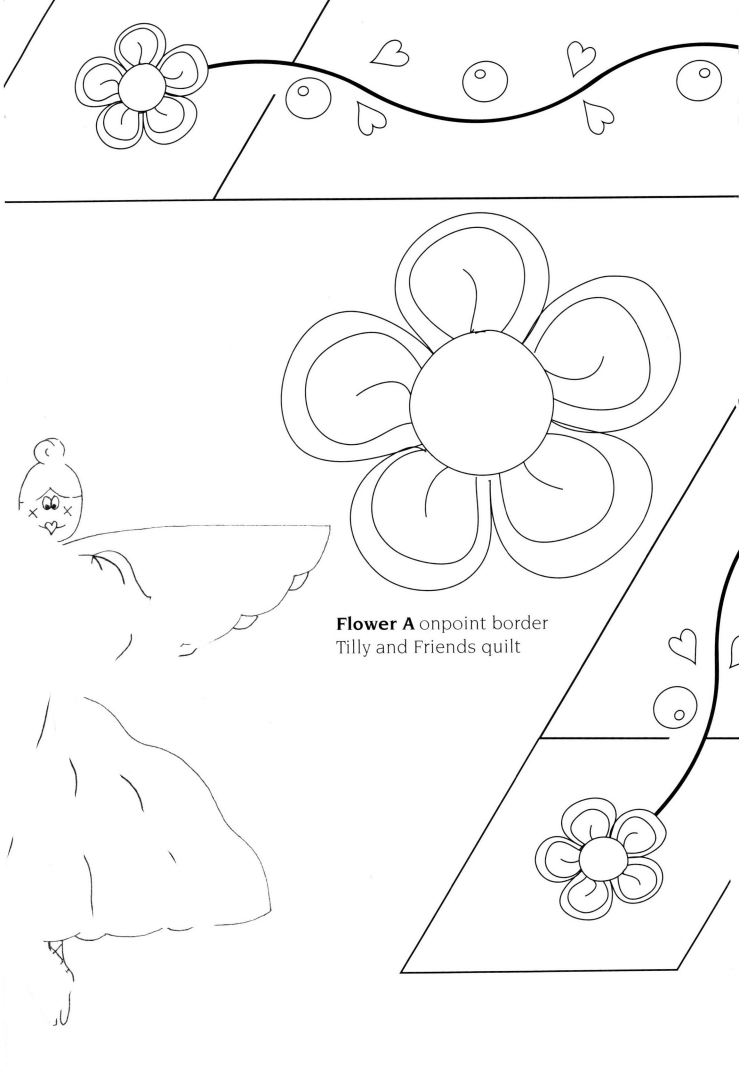

Flower A onpoint border
Tilly and Friends quilt

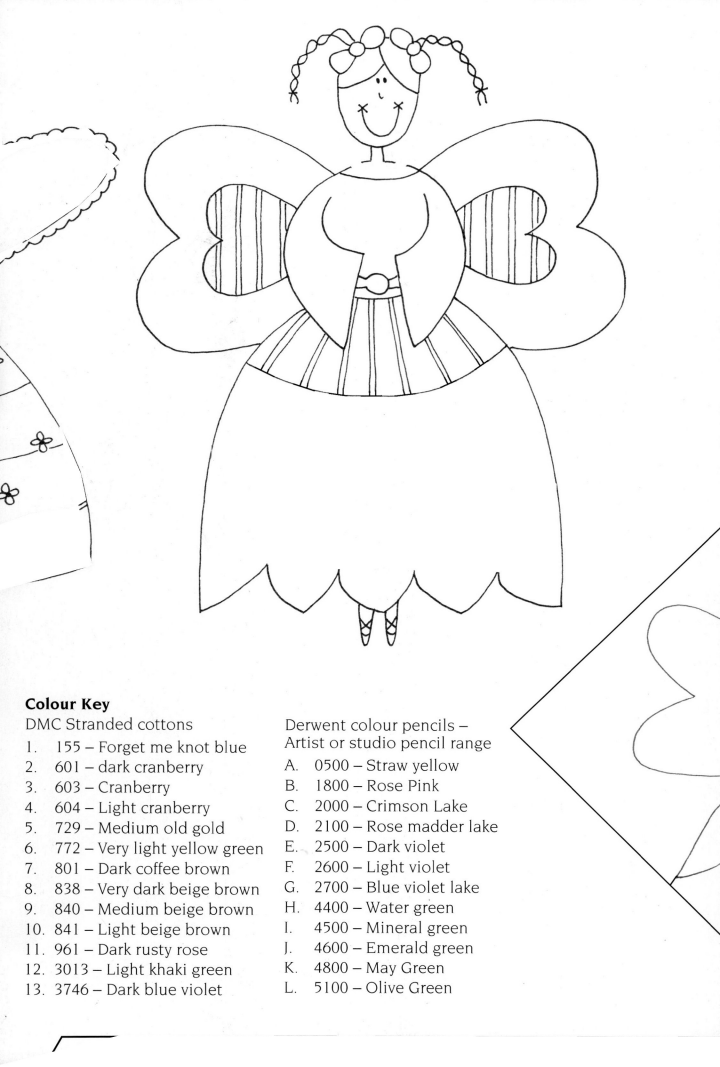

Colour Key

DMC Stranded cottons

1. 155 – Forget me knot blue
2. 601 – dark cranberry
3. 603 – Cranberry
4. 604 – Light cranberry
5. 729 – Medium old gold
6. 772 – Very light yellow green
7. 801 – Dark coffee brown
8. 838 – Very dark beige brown
9. 840 – Medium beige brown
10. 841 – Light beige brown
11. 961 – Dark rusty rose
12. 3013 – Light khaki green
13. 3746 – Dark blue violet

Derwent colour pencils –
Artist or studio pencil range

A. 0500 – Straw yellow
B. 1800 – Rose Pink
C. 2000 – Crimson Lake
D. 2100 – Rose madder lake
E. 2500 – Dark violet
F. 2600 – Light violet
G. 2700 – Blue violet lake
H. 4400 – Water green
I. 4500 – Mineral green
J. 4600 – Emerald green
K. 4800 – May Green
L. 5100 – Olive Green